DEPARTMENT OF THE NAVY
HEADQUARTERS UNITED STATES MARINE CORPS
2 NAVY ANNEX
WASHINGTON, DC 20380-1775

MCO P5720.73
ASM-4
6 Aug 96

MARINE CORPS ORDER P5720.73 W/CH 1

From: Commandant of the Marine Corps
To: Distribution List

Subj: MARINE CORPS AVIATION SUPPORT OF THE COMMUNITY RELATIONS
PROGRAM MANUAL (SHORT TITLE: MARCORAVNSPTCOMRELPRGMAN)

Ref: (a) DoDInst 5410.19 (NOTAL)
>CH 1 (b) Assistant Secretary of Defense for Public Affairs
memo of 30 Jan 1998 (NOTAL)

Encl: (1) LOCATOR SHEET

Report Required: Airshow After Action Report (Report Control
Symbol DD-5720-27), par. 2201 and App C

1. <u>Purpose</u>. To publish, per the references, regulations and
guidance concerning the use of Marine Corps aircraft and personnel
for promoting community relations and demonstrating Marine Air
capabilities through orientation/indoctrination flights.

2. <u>Cancellation</u>. MCO 5410.12.

3. <u>Background</u>. This Manual is designed to consolidate
information and regulations pertinent to Marine Corps Aviation
participation in public events, AV-8B aircraft demonstrations,
and orientation/indoctrination flights for military personnel
and civilians.

4. <u>Action</u>. The administrative procedures in this Manual are
to be used by all activities requesting Marine Aviation
participation in community relations events or programs, and as a

DISTRIBUTION STATEMENT A: Approved for public release
distribution is unlimited.

policy guide for units supporting public events, programs and orientation/indoctrination flights for military personnel and civilians.

R. D. HEARNEY
Assistant Commandant
of the Marine Corps

DISTRIBUTION: PCN 10208952800

    Copy to: 7000110 (55)
             7000016 (5)
             8145005, 7000064 (2)
             7000099, 144/8145001, 7000093, 7000190, (1)

DEPARTMENT OF THE NAVY
HEADQUARTERS UNITED STATES MARINE CORPS
2 NAVY ANNEX
WASHINGTON, DC 20380-1775

MCO P5720.73 Ch 1
ASM-4
3 Sep 01

MARINE CORPS ORDER P5720.73 Ch 1

From: Commandant of the Marine Corps
To: Distribution List

Subj: MARINE CORPS AVIATION SUPPORT OF THE COMMUNITY RELATIONS
      PROGRAM MANUAL (SHORT TITLE: MARCORAVNSPTCOMRELPRGRMAN)

1. Purpose. To direct pen changes to the basic Manual.

2. Action

    a. Add reference (b): Assistant Secretary of Defense for Public Affairs memo of 30 Jan 1998 (NOTAL).

    b. Change paragraph 1, line 2 of the basic directive to read references vice reference.

    c. In subparagraph 2103.2b, change "The CMC (ASM) may approve fly-overs off base only in observance of the five patriotic holidays:" to "Fly-overs at off base locations generally will only be approved for observance of the five patriotic holidays:".

    d. In subparagraph 2103.5, change "DoD" to "Assistant Commandant of the Marine Corps (ACMC)".

    e. In paragraph 2302.1, change "Assistant Secretary of Defense (ASD (PA))" to "Assistant Commandant of the Marine Corps (ACMC)".

    f. Change subparagraph 2302.1a to read: "The following types of demonstrations involving Marine Corps personnel, aircraft and equipment: AV-8B, parachute, helicopter rappelling/Special Patrol, Insertion, and Extraction (SPIE), air-to-air refueling, and Marine Air Ground Task Force (MAGTF) demonstrations."

    g. Delete subparagraph 2302.1b and renumber paragraphs 2302.1c through 2302.1e accordingly.

    h. Change paragraph 2302.2 to read "Responsibility to authorize aircraft participation in public events are delegated as follows:"

    i. In subparagraph 2302.2a insert "CMC (ASM) may authorize" at the beginning of the sentence.

   j. Change subparagraph 2302.2b to read: "CMC (ASM/PAC) may authorize fly-overs at events off military installations

   k. In subparagraph 2302.2c insert "CMC (ASM) may authorize" at the beginning of the sentence.

   l. In subparagraph 2302.2d insert "CMC (ASM/PAC) may authorize" at the beginning of the sentence.

   m. In subparagraph 2302.2e change entire paragraph to read "CMC (ASM/PAC) may authorize search and rescue demonstrations"

3. Summary of Changes. The changes directed by paragraphs 2a to 2m update the references and reflect changes in Assistant Secretary of Defense for Public Affairs policy concerning military aerial support functions.

4. Filing Instructions. This change will be filed immediately behind the signature page of the basic Manual.

M. J. WILLIAMS
Assistant Commandant
of the Marine Corps

DISTRIBUTION: PCN 10208952801
   Copy to: 7000110   (55)
               7000016   (5)
               8145005/7000064 (2)
               7000093,099,144,190/8145001 (1)

LOCATOR SHEET

Subj: MARINE CORPS AVIATION SUPPORT OF THE COMMUNITY RELATIONS
PROGRAM MANUAL (SHORT TITLE: MARCORAVNSPTCOMRELPRGMAN)

Location:_____
          (Indicate the location(s) of the copy(s) of this
          Manual.)

RECORD OF CHANGES

Log completed change action as indicated.

CHANGE NUMBER	DATE OF CHANGE	DATE ENTERED	SIGNATURE OF PERSON ENTERING CHANGE

MARCORAVNSPTCOMRELPRGMAN

CONTENTS

CHAPTER

CHAPTER 1

GENERAL INFORMATION

CHAPTER 1

GENERAL INFORMATION

SECTION 1: PURPOSE

1100. <u>PURPOSE</u>. The Marine Corps participates in programs
that support aerial events, static displays, and orientation
indoctrination flights. These programs keep the public, civilian
leaders and military commanders informed of the Marine
preparedness, demonstrate modern weapons systems, enhance
community and international relations, and promote the recruiting
effort. Aircraft support of public events may include specifically
designated military parachute/flight demonstration teams,
fly-overs, aerial reviews, static displays and other aerial
activities. The availability of Marine Corps aircraft and crews
for aviation events is limited by operational, training and safety
considerations and by the guidelines set forth in this Manual.

CHAPTER 1

GENERAL INFORMATION

SECTION 2: GLOSSARY

1200. DEFINITIONS

1. Aerial Event. Any occasion such as an air show, festival, official Federal Government function, or official military or civic function held on a military installation or where an Armed Forces aerial demonstration or display is either a primary or incidental attraction.

2. Aerial Demonstrations

    a. Aerial Activities. All aerial demonstrations not specifically listed below designed to portray the operational capabilities by a single or group of aircraft or personnel. Aerial activities include, but are not limited to, air-to-air refueling, helicopter flight techniques, air delivery of paratroops or equipment, assault aircraft demonstrations, tactical helicopter troop landings under simulated tactical conditions, and rappelling demonstrations.

    b. Aerial Review. A fly-over of more than four aircraft, multiple models of aircraft, or aircraft from more than one branch of service.

    c. Aircraft Demonstration. The demonstration of operational performance by a single aircraft or group of same type aircraft, not part of an officially designated flight demonstration team. Demonstrations may include, but are not limited to maximum performance takeoffs and performance record demonstrations.

    d. Flight Team Demonstration. A demonstration by the U.S. Navy Flight Demonstration Team (Blue Angels) or the U.S. Air Force Air Demonstration Squadron (Thunderbirds) or other service teams.

    e. Fly-over. A flight of no more than four aircraft of the same model from the same branch of service, making one pass only over a fixed point at a specified time, and not involving aerobatics or aircraft demonstration.

f. <u>Orientation/Indoctrination Flights</u>. Continuous flights performed within the local flying area, terminating at point of origin, carrying passengers/selected passengers for one of the following purposes:

(1) To familiarize them with the aircraft, its operation, capabilities, requirements, limitations, or concept of employment.

(2) To familiarize them with a base complex from the air for official purpose other than merely sight-seeing or goodwill.

(3) For evaluation of navigation facilities and air traffic control procedures which directly affect operations at naval air activities.

g. <u>Parachute Jump, Equipment Drop, Rappelling or Special Patrol Insertion/Extraction (SPIE) Demonstration</u>. Any parachute jump, equipment drop, rappelling or SPIE demonstration by Marine Corps personnel or aircraft taking part in public events or community relations programs.

h. <u>Parachute Team Demonstration</u>. A demonstration of free fall and precision landing techniques by the officially designated unit, the U.S. Army Golden Knights. Other military parachute teams, including individuals or groups, may be specifically authorized for such demonstrations when representing DoD.

i. <u>Weapons Demonstration</u>. Any demonstration employing or simulating the use of munitions or weapons.

3. <u>On Base</u>. An installation owned or operated by the Department of Defense (DoD) or by DoD component, such as a base, station, post, reservation, camp, fort, terminal, facility, ship, school, college. For aerial demonstrations, airspace that is under military control or joint military/civilian control is considered on base.

4. <u>Off Base</u>. Any location, other than a military installation, at or on which community relations programs might be conducted.

5. <u>Passengers</u>. Personnel who are not assigned as crew and are embarked for orientation/indoctrination flights aboard cargo/ transport aircraft.

6. Selected Passengers. Personnel who are not assigned as primary crew and are embarked for orientation/indoctrination flights either:

    a. aboard aircraft equipped with ejection seats or personal oxygen systems which are used for primary life support, or

    b. a military member or civilian employee of DoD or contractor to DoD embarked for the purpose of performing a crew duty, such as operating installed equipment or observing aircraft or crew performance when required in connection with assigned duties or contractual responsibilities.

7. Static Display. The ground display of any aircraft and its related equipment, not involving flight, taxi, or engine starts.

8. Public Tactical Demonstrations. Mass parachute jumps, aerial delivery of equipment, assault aircraft demonstrations, or tactical helicopter troop landings under simulated tactical conditions.

9. VIP. VIP's are defined as flag officers, DoD officials equal to or senior to flag officers, high-profile public figures, elected members of Congress, etc.

CHAPTER 1

GENERAL INFORMATION

SECTION 3: EVALUATION

1300. __EVALUATION__. Aviation events for which Marine Corps support is requested are evaluated using the program, sponsor, site and support criteria in SECNAVINST 5720.44. Additionally, DoD has established certain policy guidelines applicable for aviation support, and they are summarized as follows:

1. All pertinent safety regulations of DoD and the Department of Transportation (Federal Aviation Administration) will be rigidly observed and will take precedence over any or all conditions or circumstances.

2. Maximum advantage of military recruiting will be taken at public events where Armed Forces aerial demonstrations and static displays have been authorized.

3. During the hours that aircraft are actually on display or providing demonstrations before the public, qualified crewmembers will be available to explain the missions performed and answer questions for spectators.

4. Armed Forces aerial demonstrations and static displays are normally limited to 2 days in any one aviation event. However, parachute demonstrations may extend over a 3 day period. This provision may be waived when:

a. other requests for airshow support at a different location have not been previously authorized.

b. extended participation does not compromise another event because of travel time.

c. it is determined that the audience will change each day.

d. the event is of a national or international nature.

5. No two aerial demonstrations of the same type will be approved for a single event. Fly-overs may be authorized at an

event where a flight or parachute team will perform, provided
they are scheduled on days other than those authorized for the
demonstration team's performance.

6. Public events which are appropriate for Armed Forces aerial
demonstrations and static displays include dedications of airports
and airport facilities; aviation shows, expositions and fairs;
civic events which contribute to the public knowledge of Armed
Forces aviation equipment and capabilities; and events aboard
military installations. Appearances by DoD flight and parachute
demonstration teams will be approved for military installations
only in support of official open house programs.

7. Conflict of interest, implications of fraud, waste, and abuse,
and inequitable treatment are avoided when the policy of
SECNAVINST 5720.44 is enforced. Unit commanders, operations
officers, and public affairs officers at all levels are expected
to be cognizant of and comply with policies governing aerial
activities involving the public.

CHAPTER 2

MARINE CORPS PARTICIPATION AT PUBLIC EVENTS

CHAPTER 2

MARINE CORPS PARTICIPATION AT PUBLIC EVENTS

SECTION 1: AERIAL EVENTS

2100. GENERAL

1. The Marine Corps takes part in aerial events and static
displays in accordance with the procedures and policies outlined
in the references and this Manual.

a. Static displays are the primary method of Marine Corps
participation in public events and community relations programs.

b. Fly-overs are considered a secondary method of Marine
Corps participation. Each commander must evaluate all requests
for impact on safety, fuel conservation, flying hour programs,
training, public reaction, and possible benefits to the U.S.
Marine Corps.

c. The Navy Demonstration Team (Blue Angels) is the primary
unit authorized to exhibit publicly the capabilities of modern,
high performance aircraft and the high degree of skill required
to operate these aircraft.

d. The AV-8B, performing a Level III demonstration, is the
Marine Corps' primary aircraft used to exhibit publicly the
capabilities of modern high performance aircraft and the high
degree of skill required to operate these aircraft.

e. Events offering highest positive media exposure are most
desired. Presence of other USMC units, distinguished military
and civilian personages give added value.

2. A Request for Military Support, DD Form 2535 (appendix A),
for USMC participation at a multi-Service display, must be
submitted to the Office of the Assistant Secretary of Defense for
Public Affairs (OATSD-PA) at least 90 days before the event
(except for AV-8B demonstrations). Optimum lead time for static
display requests is 90 days; requests received by OATSD-PA within
30 days of the event will not be processed. Send information copy
to the CMC (PAC/ASM).

a. Request for Marine Corps aircraft only static displays must be submitted to the CMC (ASM/PAC) at least 90 days before the event. Requests received within 30 days of the event will be processed, but risk not being supported.

3. The following safety standards must be considered in planning and staging on base demonstrations:

a. At least a 2500-foot ceiling and 5-Mile visibility are required for any aerial event. The nature of the event, local area terrain, or numerous other factors may require the event commander to set higher minimums.

b. Minimum altitudes published in FAA regulations shall be followed, unless the FAA grants a certificate of waiver before the event which specifies a lower minimum altitude. If FAA authorizes a lower altitude, U.S. Marine Corps-controlled aircraft shall not be flown below the following minimum altitudes, above the highest obstruction:

(1) Aircraft Formation

(a) Fixed-wing - 800 feet above ground level (AGL)

(b) Helicopter - 500 feet AGL

(2) Single Aircraft

(a) Fixed-wing - 500 feet AGL

(b) Helicopter - 250 feet AGL

(3) All aircraft demonstrations must follow a command approved profile that specifies the minimum altitude for each maneuver.

4. For each aerial event or demonstration, there is normally a designated spectator area. The event commander will ensure that no part of the spectator area is located closer than 1500 feet of the line of flight. Participating aircraft shall not be operated over the designated spectator area. Measures must be taken to ensure all spectators remain within the designated area. Official observers and spectators must occupy only those areas designated for viewing the event. These safety criteria shall be a primary consideration when selecting spectator areas.

5. All aircraft shall be down loaded of all expendable ordnance before placing aircraft in a static display area. Permanently mounted internal weapons shall be rendered safe, according to applicable technical procedures. Only inert munitions will be placed on public display. All ordnance and munitions shall be secured to ensure safety. For aircraft equipped with an ejection seat, the seat will be secured per appropriate maintenance procedures.

6. Flight personnel assigned to participate in flight demonstrations should be those with the maximum training and experience that are available. Pilots shall demonstrate to their commanding officer that they are thoroughly familiar with the flight characteristics of the aircraft by precisely and safely performing all maneuvers that are to be demonstrated. When aircraft are required to proceed to another station or area for a demonstration, the commanding officer shall certify to the on-scene commander the pertinent qualifications of each flight crewmember.

7. No extra hazardous or unusual maneuvers shall be planned for or permitted during the demonstration. Routine maneuvers shall not be conducted in a manner that could make them hazardous (e.g., at excessively low altitudes or with excessively close interval between aircraft). Care shall be exercised in planning and conducting the demonstration to provide the maximum safety to personnel and property in the event of an accident. Weapons demonstrations are not authorized at public events.

2101. SPONSOR REQUIREMENT

1. The Marine Corps' support of aerial events shall normally be at no additional cost to the Government. The Request for Military Aerial Support, DD Form 2535, will be utilized to determine the ability and willingness of the sponsors, military or civilian, to defray costs of military participation. Expenses incurred by sponsors include the following:

    a. Meals consumed by participants when required to be away from station during normal meal hours, to include meals en route to distant locations.

b. Lodging costs when overnight billeting is required. It is the responsibility of the sponsor to locate and reserve billeting, whether in military or civilian facilities.

c. Local transportation between event site and billeting location and, for persons traveling by aircraft, transportation to and from the airport.

2. Although monetary reimbursement for participants in the amount equivalent to the per diem rate in the area of the event is preferred, sponsors may defray these expenses in kind by arranging for group rates at hotels, buffet-type feeding and courtesy transportation. Supporting commands must determine in advance of the event that the exact details of the sponsor's logistical support are understood and mutually agreeable.

3. Marines participating in events away from their home station will be issued permissive travel orders. In the unlikely event that sponsors renege on their commitments to adequately defray expenses, Marines who participate in public events away from their home station are encouraged to carry sufficient cash to pay for their own meals and lodging, if required. Additionally, if transportation delays necessitate additional nights lodging and added meals, the sponsors cannot be expected to fund for these unforeseen expenses. Headquarters Marine Corps will make a reasonable effort to determine that sponsors understand their obligations to provide support prior to authorizing commands to participate in events outside their community relations area of responsibility. If Marines are forced to pay out-of-pocket expenses through no fault of their own, a claim for reimbursement may be submitted to the CMC (PAC) stating the circumstances that justify reimbursement and the nature and amount of costs incurred.

4. There is no requirement for sponsors to reimburse the supporting unit for fuel consumed; however, if fuel cannot be obtained at military contract prices at the site of the event, the sponsor must pay all costs, including transportation and handling, if necessary, over military contract prices. Pilots will make every effort to lessen the financial burden on the sponsor by purchasing minimum fuel from non-contract vendors. Use the closest military installation for fueling before arrival and after departure from the event site when feasible.

5. Additional support required from the sponsors before the aerial demonstrations can be approved may include the following:

    a. A recent aerial photograph, taken vertically from an altitude of 5,000 feet or higher.

    b. An ambulance and a doctor on the site during flight, parachute and rappelling/SPIE demonstrations and certain other aerial activities as determined in advance.

    c. Mobile fire fighting, crash and ground-to-air communications equipment at the demonstration site.

    d. Security for aircraft during their stay.

6. Sponsors are required to obtain an FAA waiver for any public demonstration by military aircraft or parachutists. The final authorization for such demonstrations hinges upon the sponsor securing this waiver far enough in advance to permit adequate planning (normally no later than 60 days prior to the event). No waiver is required for static displays, but helicopters landing at areas other than operating airports for static displays may require advance FAA clearance.

2102. STATIC DISPLAYS

1. In no case will fixed-wing aircraft be towed or taxied to non-airfield areas, such as shopping malls, for static display.

2. Helicopters may be authorized for landing and static display off base for the purpose of participation in a public event. Due to the limited number of these events that can be supported, requests should be carefully screened. At off base areas, aircraft will not be started, taxied, or flown within 100 yards of spectators. Aircraft must be in position before spectators arrive.

3. When requesting aircraft for static display, the sponsor is responsible for ensuring availability of mobile fire fighting equipment, medical services, spectator control, and FAA approval, when required.

2103. <u>FLY-OVERS</u>

1. Fly-overs performed at public events are conducted as public affairs activities in support of community relation programs of the Department of Defense and the Marine Corps. Aviation participation in community events such as patriotic observances and air shows is encouraged; however, it must be within prescribed policy limitations. Fly-over policy is established in consideration of safety, availability of assets, public demand, unit missions, event focus, appropriateness of participation, and equitable consideration for all eligible requests.

2. Fly-overs will be approved only for the following occasions:

     a. When directed by the Office of the Secretary of Defense.

>CH 1 b. Fly-overs at off base locations generally will only be approved for observance of the five patriotic holidays: Armed Forces Day, Memorial Day, Independence Day, POW/MIA Recognition Day, and Veterans Day. Flights must be within 7 days of the actual holiday and have a formal observance/ceremony for the patriotic holiday in order to qualify.

3. Fly-overs for the five patriotic holidays are limited to one to four aircraft of the same model from a single service making a single pass.

4. Missing man formations are not authorized for community relations events, but reserved for individual funeral/memorial services for designated active duty personnel or dignitaries of the Armed Force and Federal Government.

>CH 1 5. Fly-overs involving aircraft from more than one service or more than one type of aircraft fall under the category of an aerial review. Joint service (more than one service) aerial reviews conducted on or off base and single service aerial reviews (fly-overs by more than one model of aircraft) require Assistant Commandant of the Marine Corps (ACMC) approval. Aerial reviews are carefully scrutinized and usually considered only for the most significant ceremonial occasions (i.e., Ceremonies directed by executive order, retirements for cabinet level officials).

6. The CMC (ASM/PAC) will coordinate with CHINFO and OATSD-PA to ensure an event is not being supported by more than one service.

2104. AV-8B HARRIER DEMONSTRATIONS

1. The AV-8B Harrier is in heavy demand for participation in air
shows and other public events due to its unique performance
capabilities. Because the Harrier is a tactical aircraft organic
to units that are committed to demanding operational requirements,
the majority of requests for AV-8B support of public events must
be declined. Stringent measures are taken to ensure that the
approved AV-8B demonstration schedule is based on careful
appraisal of all requests.

2. Requests for AV-8B static displays will be processed through
the same channels as for other types aircraft.

3. AV-8B demonstrations in support of public events consists of
two aircraft, one of which is utilized for a 10-15 minute flight
demonstration and another for static display and backup. The
following levels of flying air shows are as follows:

    a. Level I

        (1) Two to four aircraft formation fly-over

        (2) 500 ft/250 knots or as restricted by FAA coordinator

        (3) Absolute minimum of 200 ft

        (4) A section of aircraft can do a slow pass in the
landing configuration at optimum angle of attack at 500 ft* with a
minimum of 200 ft if authorized by the FAA coordinator.

    b. Level II

        (1) One aircraft (limited show due to: weather, time, FAA
limits, airfield or grandstand limitations)

        (2) Aircraft enters overhead 500 ft/250 knots or at a
speed approved by written FAA agreement. Break to arrive in a
landing configuration at the 180. Decelerate to hover in front of
the audience. Back up in a hover. STOP. Turn 90 degrees to

    * A RVTO or VTO to a hover can be substituted for the
overhead entry to the field.

face audience. Do translation left and right. STOP. Do a 360 degrees spot turn. STOP. Turn to align aircraft into wind and execute a vertical landing. If a vertical landing is not appropriate due to landing surface composition, conduct a rolling vertical landing.

    c. <u>Level III</u>

       (1) Taxi out in front of the grandstand for a short take off (STO). Following a STO do a 80 degrees climbing turn away from grandstand. Reverse turn 260 degrees to fly over the runway at 500 ft in a high speed pass. A minimum altitude of 200 ft and speed above 250 knots requires FAA approval. Turn 80 degrees away from stands and then reverse turn 260 degrees while transitioning to the landing configuration. Come to a hover in front of the stands. Back up 50 to 100 ft. STOP. Turn to face the crowd. Translate left and then right 50 to 100 ft. STOP. Do a 360 degrees spot turn. STOP. Turn 90 degrees to align with landing area and do a rolling vertical landing. STOP. (A vertical landing can be done if the runway surface permits.) Do a vertical or a rolling vertical take off into the wind (but not over the crowd) to a steep climb out. Turn downwind at 1000 ft for a 180 position. Decelerate from the 180 to do a vertical or rolling vertical landing in front of the grandstand. Taxi clear and shut down.

    d. Special requirements for air show preparation:

       (1) Pilots leading level one or flying level two or three demonstrations will have a minimum of 500 hours in the AV-8.

       (2) A maximum of four demonstration pilots per squadron will be nominated by the Squadron Commanding Officer for approval by the Group Commander.

       (3) The Squadron Commanding Officer will view a satisfactory practice of the appropriate level two or three air show within one week of the scheduled performance.

       (4) A practice should be accomplished, if possible, at the air show site prior to the scheduled show.

(5) For air shows that require the aircraft to remain over night, one AV-8B maintenance man should be provided for aircraft preparation.

(6) The pilot of the backup aircraft shall narrate the demonstration.

4. Site Selection:

a. AV-8B public flight demonstrations are scheduled by a committee which is convened at Headquarters Marine Corps during February of each year. The committee is composed of representatives from Public Affairs, Recruiting, Legislative Affairs and Aviation. The FMF commands are invited to send representatives and/or recommendations.

b. The final schedule is submitted for approval by the Assistant Commandant of the Marine Corps, and no changes will be made in the approved schedule without their concurrence.

c. Except for the Joint Services Open House at Andrews AFB, MD, and airshows at Marine Corps Air Stations, the following criteria is used as a guide for selecting the sites and dates for AV-8B demonstrations:

(1) Demonstrations will be scheduled with due consideration of exercise, readiness training, operational commitments.

(2) Demonstrations shall not be scheduled at events where the Blue Angels or Thunderbirds are performing.

(3) To enhance the benefits of exposure, the event must:

(a) be open to the public

(b) have a minimum forecast crowd of at least 10,000

(c) have an active USMC recruiting program planned

(d) be open to the news media.

(4) Sites at altitudes greater than 3500 feet mean sea level (MSL) will not be considered.

(5) Flight demonstration aircraft must operate from suitable airfields or the site of the event must be within reasonable distance of a staging base. In the latter case, performances are seldom authorized since the recruiting potential is significantly reduced.

(6) Unless otherwise noted, locations where the AV-8B has not been previously displayed will be given priority.

5. The unusual design of the AV-8B aircraft creates additional support requirements for event sponsors. An AV-8B Support Requirements Checklist (appendix B) will be enclosed with letters sent by the CMC (PA) to sponsors confirming AV-8B participation. They must be completed, signed and forwarded to the participating aircraft group no later than 3 weeks prior to the event date. The event sponsor must provide round trip commercial transportation between home station and event site for support personnel for the AV-8B Demonstrations. The sponsor's inability to meet all of these requirements may result in cancellation of AV-8B participation.

2105. <u>PARACHUTE DEMONSTRATIONS</u>

1. <u>Sport Parachute Clubs</u>

a. Authorized parachute clubs located aboard military installations are entirely voluntary, off-duty and self-supporting groups receiving neither appropriated nor non-appropriated funding. Commanders can make available Navy and Marine Corps equipment and facilities, including military aircraft, to established military sports parachute clubs.

b. Eligibility to join and participate with the clubs is restricted to active duty military personnel. Proficient parachutists are authorized to make exhibition jumps for the purposes of entertainment and demonstration of techniques. Prior coordination with FAA as well as state and local officials is required well in advance of each jump. Exhibition parachute jumps by military clubs also require approval by the U.S. Parachute Association Area Safety Officer.

c. Although jumps by parachutists from military clubs have been used to enhance public events and the recruiting effort, their participation is considered unofficial. Requests for their support may be submitted to the club leaders. Requests for aircraft jump platforms will be originated by the club. The use of Marine Corps aircraft to support parachute club participation at public events will be authorized only at military or joint-use military/civilian airfields.

2. Marine Corps Parachutists

    a. Marine Corps parachutists authorized to participate in jumps/skydiving demonstrations in support of public events are limited to personnel who have completed military parachute training at Ft. Benning, Georgia, and who are currently serving in billets that require continuous parachute proficiency. The supervision of a qualified jump master is also required during the demonstration and any rehearsals that may be required. Those individuals designated to perform the parachute demonstration shall have completed a practice parachute exercise within 7 days of the scheduled event.

    b. Official Marine Corps parachute demonstrations at public events in the civilian domain are not authorized. Requests for Marine Corps parachute demonstrations will normally not be approved if another official military parachute team is scheduled to perform.

3. Special Requirements

    a. Parachuting will be authorized only at military/joint use airfields, military installations and military training sites.

    b. Marine Corps aircraft will not be used as jump platforms for parachute clubs unless the club is sponsored by a military service.

    c. The event commander is responsible for ensuring the eligibility and qualifications of the parachutists, for providing mobile fire fighting equipment, medical services, spectator control, and that FAA approval has been obtained by the event sponsor, when required.

2106. <u>HELICOPTER RAPPELLING DEMONSTRATIONS</u>

1. Marine Corps helicopter rappelling demonstrations can greatly enhance a public event. Rappelling demonstrations, especially when used in conjunction with a SPIE rig, can vividly illustrate the Marine Corps mission by showing the air-ground team in action. Rappelling demonstrations are also a useful recruiting tool that attract attention and stimulate the sense of adventure in potential enlistees.

2. Helicopter rappelling demonstrations at public events will be authorized only at military or joint-use military/civilian airfields. Although no written criteria are established on which the qualifications of rappellers may be based, it is the responsibility of the commander of the unit designated to provide the rappelling team to ensure that the team members are qualified and have recent and/or extensive helicopter rappelling experience. The commander of the rappelling team's unit will coordinate with the supporting aircraft unit to determine the need for a rehearsal prior to a public demonstration.

2107. <u>MAGTF AND TACTICAL DEMONSTRATIONS</u>

1. Demonstrations designed to show Marine Corps tactical doctrine and coordination of the Air-Ground team are limited to events sponsored by the Marine Corps held aboard Marine Corps Air Stations, Air Facilities, Bases, and Installations. These demonstrations may be approved by Force Commanders. These demonstrations, except those scheduled as part of a regular training program, are not authorized for public events.

2108. <u>AIRCRAFT DEMONSTRATIONS</u>. Other than the AV-8B demonstrations, the Marine Corps does not perform aircraft demonstrations.

CHAPTER 2

MARINE CORPS PARTICIPATION AT PUBLIC EVENTS

SECTION 2: RESPONSIBILITIES

2200. <u>RESPONSIBILITIES</u>

1. <u>Headquarters Marine Corps</u>

a. Evaluate requests for all off base aerial events and static displays to determine eligibility, feasibility, and extent of participation.

b. Advise subordinate commands of approved events and solicit their support. Support of approved events shall not interfere with operational commitments or scheduled training programs.

c. Publish a monthly Marine Corps Aviation Support for Public Events message.

2. <u>Force Commanders (COMMARFORPAC, COMMARFORLANT, COMMARFORRES)</u>.

a. Evaluate requests for all aerial events on Marine Corps installations, bases, and air stations to determine feasibility and extent of participation per the provisions of SECNAVINST 5720.44.

b. Coordinate with the CMC (ASM) and other agencies to determine the extent of authorized participation.

c. Advise subordinate commands of approved events and solicit their support. Support of approved events shall not interfere with operational commitments or scheduled training programs.

d. Notify the CMC (ASM) when subordinate command(s) commit resources, specifying the number and type of aircraft and/or equipment.

3.   Subordinate Commands (All Wings, Divisions, Brigades).   Each command that takes part in or supports an event:

     a.   Shall appoint a command project officer to plan, coordinate, brief all events, and act as the event commander.

     b.   Provide required resources to complete the mission.

     c.   Prepare either a Letter of Instruction (LOI) or an operations plan and/or order(s) in support of the event outlining all aspects of the event.

     d.   Provide support facilities for the event.   The participating command will arrange for support beyond the capability of the event site.

     e.   Ensure that aircraft and equipment are representative of the U.S. Marine Corps.

     f.   Ensure aircrew, ground personnel and participants are selected on the basis of military bearing, ability to communicate with the public, and knowledge of equipment.   Further ensure that proper flight or duty uniform/equipment is worn.   May be delegated to the participating unit.

     g.   Ensure event sponsor coordinates all public event aerial activity with the Federal Aviation Agency (FAA), through the regional representative.   May be delegated to the participating unit.

     h.   Ensure proper performance specification placards are available for each aircraft or equipment involved in the static display.

     i.   Review subordinate command(s) operations plans for each event and ensure all safety aspects of the event have been reviewed.

4.   The event commander shall be a designated naval aviator or naval flight officer for all aerial events who shall act as the on scene commander responsible for the overall safety and conduct of the event, or static display.   Responsibilities will include but not be limited to:

     a.   Making the "go" or "no go" weather decision.

   b. Ensuring that required FAA coordination and approval has
been obtained by event sponsor.

   c. Ensuring that all mission details are operationally
feasible and all necessary coordination is effected to ensure a
safe execution of all stages of the scheduled event.

2201. <u>REPORTS</u>. Commands authorized to provide aerial support of
public events shall submit an after action report to the CMC
(PAC/ASM) no later than 30 days following the event. A sample
format is provided in appendix C. Report Control Symbol
DD-5720-27 has been assigned to this report.

CHAPTER 2

MARINE CORPS PARTICIPATION IN PUBLIC EVENTS

SECTION 3: REQUEST AND APPROVAL

2300. <u>REQUESTS FOR AERIAL SUPPORT</u>

1. <u>Demonstration Teams</u>. Office of the Assistant Secretary of
Defense (OASD)(PA)) hosts a scheduling conference in mid-December
each year to prepare the official flight and parachute team's
performance schedules for the following year. All requests for
these teams (Thunderbirds, Blue Angels, and Golden Knights)
originated by Marine Corps commands must be received by the CMC
(PAC) no later than 30 September of each year. Requests are to be
submitted using the Request for Military Aerial Support (DD Form
2535) contained in appendix A. Schedules are normally released
during December.

2. <u>Other Military Services</u>

     a. <u>Navy Parachute Teams</u>. The U.S. Navy Parachute Teams East
and West, located in Norfolk, Virginia, and Coronado, California
(nicknamed the "Chuting Stars") are scheduled by the Commander,
Navy Recruiting Command. Requests may be forwarded to the CMC
(PAC) no later than 90 days prior to the date of the event.

     b. <u>Allied Aircraft</u>. Requests for Canadian aircraft for
participation in open house events may be forwarded to the CMC
(PAC) for submission through proper channels. When DoD learns of
other Allied aircraft that may be in the United States and are
available for public events, request procedures will be announced.

     c. Requests for aerial participation of other Armed Forces
aircraft at Marine Corps Installation open houses may be submitted
directly to the major command with the capability to provide the
support. There is no requirement to route these requests through
the CMC.

2301. <u>REQUEST CHANNELS</u>

    a. Requests for Marine Corps aviation support originated by
civilian sponsors may be submitted to the nearest Marine Corps
activity to be forwarded through proper channels. Requests that
clearly do not meet the established criteria for support or for
which the sponsors are unable or unwilling to meet their
responsibilities will not be forwarded to higher authority.
Rather, the sponsor will be notified as soon as possible of
requirements that must be met before the request can be considered.
Recruiting commands that forward civilian requests will include an
estimate of recruiting value that may be gained by participation.

    b. Requests for aerial participation in events in the public
domain that are received by the CMC (ASM/PAC), and that meet
established DoD support criteria, will be relayed to the
appropriate Marine Forces commander requesting comments on ability
to provide the requested support. Marine Corps aviation commands
are encouraged to participate as operational, training and
maintenance requirements permit. Consideration should be given to
incorporating public support into routinely scheduled cross-country
or training flights, if feasible. When the CMC has received a
response from a command stating that a public event will be
supported, participation will be authorized on a basis of non-
interference with operational and training requirements.

    c. Requests received by HQMC for support of military open
house events and in direct support of Marine Corps recruiting
programs (non-public events) will be forwarded to the appropriate
Marine Forces commander for action.

2302. <u>APPROVAL AUTHORITY</u>

>CH 1 1. The Assistant Commandant of the Marine Corps (ACMC)
will approve Armed Forces aerial demonstrations in support of
public programs as follows:

>CH 1 a. The following types of demonstrations involving Marine
 Corps personnel, aircraft and equipment: AV-8B, parachute,
 helicpoter rapelling/Special Patrol, Insertion, and Extraction
 (SPIE), air-to-air refueling, and Marine Air Ground Task Force
 (MAGTF) demonstrations.

   b. Aerial reviews involving more than one military service held on a military installation and all aerial reviews held elsewhere.

   c. Aerial demonstrations held outside the United States which are not within a unified or specified command area of responsibility.

   d. Other aerial activities held off a military installation, except as provided in paragraphs 2302.2 and 2302.3 below.

>CH 1 2. Responsibility to authorize aircraft participation in public events are designated as follows:

>CH 1 a. CMC (ASM) may authorize fly-overs for events on military installations.

>CH 1 b. CMC (ASM/PAC) may authorize fly-overs at events off military installations for civic sponsored observances of Armed Forces Day, Memorial Day, Independence Day and Veterans Day, except in the National Capital area.

>CH 1 c. Fly-overs for military funerals for rated/designated aviation personnel of the Armed Forces.

>CH 1 d. CMC (ASM/PAC) may authorize aircraft static displays held off military installations.

>CH 1 e. CMC (ASM/PAC) may authorize search and rescue demonstrations involving Marine Corps personnel, aircraft and equipment: AV-8B, search and rescue, parachute, helicopter rappelling/Special Patrol, Insertion and Extraction (SPIE),

3. COMMARFORPAC, COMMARFORLANT, and COMMARFORRES may approve static displays and aircraft demonstrations aboard Marine Corps installations. Additionally, they will:

   a. Evaluate requests for aerial events and coordinate with the CMC (ASM/PA) and other agencies to determine feasibility and extent of participation

   b. Advise subordinate commands of approved events and solicit their support

    c. Submit a request to participate in aerial events to the CMC (ASM/PA). Include the event name, location, and number and type aircraft.

CHAPTER 3

ORIENTATION/INDOCTRINATION FLIGHTS

CHAPTER 3

ORIENTATION/INDOCTRINATION FLIGHTS

SECTION 1: GENERAL INFORMATION

3100. <u>BACKGROUND</u>. Orientation/indoctrination flights are used
to give designated individuals and the public an opportunity to
develop an increased understanding of the roles and missions of
various aviation assets. Flights must be beneficial to the Marine
Corps and the Department of Defense.

3101. <u>ELIGIBLE PERSONNEL</u>

1. Military personnel on active duty and DoD employees when such
flights would improve job performance and be in the best interest
of the Marine Corps.

2. FAA personnel as specified in OPNAVINST 3710.7.

3. Foreign personnel, military or civilian, who require
orientation/indoctrination flights in military aircraft for
scientific research, development, test and evaluation purposes and
to support the military assistance program (MAP) and foreign
military sales program (FMS).

4. Persons who because of their group affiliation are authorized
orientation/indoctrination flights by separate directives (i.e.,
senior scout program, Civil Air Patrol, ROTC and NJROTC students,
and other such groups as may be designated by the CNO).

5. Influential persons who because of their position can help
public awareness, understanding, and appreciation of the Marine
Corps and its mission (i.e., VIP's, members of Congress and
persons affiliated with the news media and entertainment
personalities). It is not intended that flights of this nature
be scheduled in an effort to engender good will or to be tendered
as a reward for unusual service to the Marine Corps.

6. Foreign military personnel while participating in bilateral or
multinational exercises.

7. Candidates for programs leading to duty under flight orders when necessary for determining applicant suitability.

3102. FLIGHT LIMITATIONS AND RESTRICTIONS

1. In no case shall orientation/indoctrination flights in Marine Corps aircraft be conducted to provide point to point transportation.

2. Only highly qualified flight personnel shall be selected to conduct orientation/indoctrination flights. NATOPS instructors will give orientation/indoctrination flights to selected passengers occupying a crew position.

3. Flights involving disclosure of classified information to foreign nationals require compliance with provisions of OPNAVINST 5510.48.

4. Orientation/indoctrination flights involving third nation nationals into or over foreign countries will not be approved unless confirmation of entry clearance has been received from foreign governments concerned.

5. Formation flying shall not be performed unless required for specific purpose.

6. Flights in high performance jet aircraft shall not be approved except when the specific aircraft utilized is integral to the orientation/indoctrination flight purpose.

7. Physical and survival training requirements as outlined in paragraph 3103 are met.

8. Flights shall be conducted at no additional cost to the Government and are not to interfere with operations and training of the organization providing subject flight.

3103. PHYSICAL AND SURVIVAL TRAINING REQUIREMENTS

1. Physical and Survival Training requirements:

a. A current flight physical is required for selected passengers. Use of medical screening (see OPNAVINST 3710.7) by non-DoD personnel required at their own expense.

b. A current flight physical is required for passengers who occupy a crew position.

c. Naval Aviation Physiology Training (NAPTP), NP8/NP3, is required for flights in non-cargo/transport type aircraft.

d. Naval Aviation Water Survival Training (NAWSTP), N3, is required for any extended over water flights in non-cargo/ transport type aircraft.

e. The pilot in command shall ensure that passengers and selected passengers are thoroughly briefed prior to flight on use of available oxygen systems and survival equipment; and on procedures for ditching, crash landing and bailout.

2. Waivers:

a. The requirement for a flight physical for passengers or selected passengers may be waived provided the individual has a current physical which is reviewed by a flight surgeon prior to any physiology training, water survival training, or flight.

b. Physiology training waivers for orientation/ indoctrination flights in aircraft equipped with ejection seats and/or personal oxygen systems which are used for primary life support will not be granted.

c. Waivers for water survival training, N3, may be granted provided the orientation/indoctrination flight is conducted over land.

CHAPTER 3

ORIENTATION/INDOCTRINATION FLIGHTS

SECTION 2:   NON-CREWMEMBER ORIENTATION/INDOCTRINATION FLIGHT
PROGRAM

3200. PURPOSE. This program is to introduce the ground commander
to the complexities of aviation, the many facets of coordination
and communication required to execute a mission, and to provide
commanders with a better understanding of the critical balance
between safety and mission accomplishment.

3201. PROGRAM ADMINISTRATION

1. Flights will be made available, on a voluntary basis, to
Commanders at the battalion level and above.

2. Flights are authorized on a not-to-interfere basis in any
multi-crew seat configured aircraft.

3. Flights should be air-to-ground missions for attack type
aircraft. Flights in cargo/transport type aircraft should
represent a typical assault mission profile.

4. If possible, flights should be conducted in conjunction with
a ground exercise in order to provide the Commander with a greater
appreciation of the coordination and communications required to
execute a mission.

3202. RESTRICTION AND REQUIREMENTS

1. Flight limitations and restrictions of paragraph 3102 above
apply.

2. Non-crewmembers will not occupy any crew seat during flights
conducted at night or with troops/passengers embarked.

3. NVG flights will be flown during "high light" conditions
(lux of .0022 or greater). A day orientation/indoctrination
flight must be flown prior to any night flight (flights need not
be flown on the same day).

4. The number of orientation/indoctrination flights provided to any individual will not exceed three (3). Only one (1) night flight is authorized.

5. Non-crewmembers receiving orientation/indoctrination flights are not authorized to control the aircraft.

6. Non-crewmembers will receive a complete flight brief by the pilot in command to include not only NATOPS and safety items, but also a brief on the nature and conduct of the mission. Flights will be conducted within the guidelines of the appropriate aircraft NATOPS.

7. No additional funding will be provided to support this program.

8. Physical and survival training requirements as outlined in paragraph 3103 will be met.

9. Approving authorities must use caution to avoid any perception that this program is anything other than a dedicated training effort to enhance the effectiveness of Marine commanders.

CHAPTER 3

ORIENTATION/INDOCTRINATION FLIGHTS

SECTION 3: APPROVAL AUTHORITY

3300. APPROVAL AUTHORITY

1. Headquarters Marine Corps, Deputy Chief of Staff for Aviation is the approval authority for selected passengers to receive orientation/indoctrination flights in high performance jet aircraft (F/A-18D, TAV-8B, EA-6B/A-6, TA-4), aircraft with ejection seats and/or personal oxygen systems, or to occupy a crew position. (Except for flights conducted as part of the Non-Crewmember Orientation/Indoctrination Flight Program.)

2. The COMMARFORLANT, COMMARFORPAC, COMMARFORRES, and Commanding Officer, Marine Weapons and Tactics Squadron 1 (for Ground Combat students assigned to the Weapons and Tactics Instructor Course) are delegated authority to approve orientation/indoctrination flights conducted as part of the Non-Crewmember Orientation/ Indoctrination Flight Program outlined in section 2 of this chapter.

3. The COMMARFORLANT, COMMARFORPAC and COMMARFORRES are delegated authority to approve orientation/indoctrination flights for the following passengers aboard USMC cargo/transport aircraft within CONUS:

    a. U.S. military personnel on active duty or on active duty for training.

    b. Foreign military personnel who possess proper base/ installation visitation authorization.

    c. Foreign civilians assigned to a NATO headquarters and who possess a base/installation visitation authorization.

    d. U.S. citizens except for spouses of government personnel, key non-DoD federal officials, and members of Congress and their staffs.

4.   The COMMARFORLANT and COMMARFORPAC are authorized to approve orientation/indoctrination flights aboard cargo/transport aircraft for foreign nationals (military and civilian) within their respective overseas areas of responsibility.

5.   The CMC, Aviation Support Manpower and Safety Division will be an information/copy to/E-Mail addressee on all correspondence which approves an orientation/indoctrination flight aboard Marine Corps aircraft, to include flights conducted as part of the Non-Crewmember Orientation/Indoctrination Flight Program.

DD FORM 2535: REQUEST FOR MILITARY AERIAL SUPPORT

REQUEST FOR MILITARY AERIAL SUPPORT ALL EVENT SPONSORS MUST READ THE INSTRUCTIONS ON PAGE 4 BEFORE COMPLETING THIS FORM.	DOD REQUEST NUMBER	Form Approved OMB No. 0704-0290 Expires Jun 30, 1997

Public reporting burden for this collection of information is estimated to average 30 minutes per response, including the time for reviewing instructions, searching existing data sources, gathering and maintaining the data needed, and completing and reviewing the collection of information. Send comments regarding this burden estimate or any other aspect of this collection of information, including suggestions for reducing this burden, to Department of Defense, Washington Headquarters Services, Directorate for Information Operations and Reports, 1215 Jefferson Davis Highway, Suite 1204, Arlington, VA 22202-4302, and to the Office of Management and Budget, Paperwork Reduction Project (0704-0290), Washington, DC 20503.
PLEASE DO NOT RETURN YOUR FORM TO EITHER OF THESE ADDRESSES. SEND YOUR COMPLETED FORM TO THE ADDRESS ON PAGE 4.

SECTION I - ACTIVITY

1. CATEGORY REQUESTED (X and complete as applicable)	(1) DATE OF EVENT (YYMMMDD)	(2) TYPE AIRCRAFT REQUESTED		(3) MILITARY SERVICE REQUESTED	
		ANY (X)	SPECIFIC (Optional)	ALL (X)	SPECIFIC (Optional)
a. FLYOVER (See paragraph 4 of Instructions)					
b. STATIC DISPLAY (See paragraph 5 of Instructions)					
c. SINGLE AIRCRAFT DEMONSTRATION (See pars. 7 of Instructions)					
d. OTHER (Specify)					

e. AERIAL DEMONSTRATION TEAM (X all requested. See Instructions.)	(a) PRIMARY DATE (YYMMMDD)	(b) ALTERNATE DATE(S) (YYMMMDD)	(c) I WILL CONSIDER ANY DATE DURING AIR SHOW SEASON (X one)
U.S. ARMY GOLDEN KNIGHTS			
U.S. NAVY BLUE ANGELS			YES
U.S. AIR FORCE THUNDERBIRDS			NO

SECTION II - EVENT AND SITE INFORMATION

2.a. EVENT TITLE			
b. SITE OF EVENT	c. CITY AND STATE	d. SITE ELEVATION (Feet above sea level)	e. RUNWAY LENGTH X WIDTH

f. ARRESTING GEAR (X one) YES NO	g. TYPE OF SITE (i.e., airport, park, lake, etc.)

3. EVENT SITE CERTIFICATION (To be completed by airport manager or agent exercising authority for site use)
I certify that an agreement has been made with the sponsoring organization indicated in Section II to use the event site indicated in 2.b. above.

a. NAME (Last, First, Middle Initial)	b. TITLE	c. TELEPHONE NO. (Include area code)
d. SIGNATURE		e. DATE SIGNED (YYMMMDD)

4. INCLUSIVE DATES OF EVENT (YYMMMDD)	5. IS THERE CIVILIAN AVIATION/AERIAL PARTICIPATION PLANNED FOR THE EVENT? (X one)	YES NO

6. ATTENDANCE		7. PLANNED MEDIA COVERAGE (X as applicable)	
a. PROJECTED	b. PRIOR EVENT	TELEVISION	PRINT
		RADIO	NONE

SECTION III - SPONSOR INFORMATION

8. LOCAL SPONSORING ORGANIZATION	b. TYPE (X one)
a. NAME	PROFIT NONPROFIT

9. AVIATION POINT OF CONTACT FOR THIS EVENT			
a. (X one) MR.	MS. OTHER	b. NAME (Last, First, Middle Initial)	c. RANK (If military)

d. ADDRESS			
(1) NUMBER AND STREET/SUITE NUMBER	(2) CITY	(3) STATE	(4) ZIP CODE

e. TELEPHONE NO. (Include area code)	f. ALTERNATE TELEPHONE NO. (Include area code or DSN if military)	g. FAX NO. (Include area code)

DD FORM 2535, AUG 94 (EG)	PREVIOUS EDITION WILL BE USED.	Page 1 of 4 Pages Designed using Perform Pro, WHS/DIOR, Aug 94

SECTION III - SPONSOR INFORMATION (Continued)	YES	NO
10. IS EVENT OFFICIALLY SUPPORTED BY LOCAL GOVERNMENT (X one)		
11. WILL YOU PROVIDE POST-EVENT REPORT ON REQUEST? (X one)		
12. DOES SPONSORING ORGANIZATION SPECIFICALLY EXCLUDE PERSONS FROM MEMBERSHIP BASED UPON RACE, RELIGION, SEX OR COLOR? (X one)		
13. WILL ALL ASPECTS OF THIS EVENT BE AVAILABLE TO ALL PERSONS WITHOUT REGARD TO RACE, RELIGION, SEX OR COLOR? (X one)		
14. WILL THE EVENT BE OPEN TO THE GENERAL PUBLIC? (X one)		

SECTION IV - FEDERAL AVIATION ADMINISTRATION (FAA) COORDINATION (Airspace Coordination)

For this event to be considered for U.S. military support, the sponsor MUST have this section completed by the Flight Standards District Office responsible for controlling the aerial activities at the event site.

For events where the airspace falls under the purview of the United States Department of Transportation, Federal Aviation Administration (FAA) coordination is required for all U.S. military aviation activities described in Section I except aircraft static displays. THE SPONSOR WILL FORWARD THIS DOCUMENT, WITH SECTIONS I THROUGH III AND SECTIONS V THROUGH VII COMPLETED, TO THE FLIGHT STANDARDS DISTRICT OFFICE (FSDO) HAVING JURISDICTION OVER THE SITE. After completion of Section IV by the FSDO, form will be returned to the sponsor for submission to DoD. Sponsors will allow a minimum of 45 days for FAA review and completion.

15. FLIGHT STANDARDS DISTRICT OFFICE REVIEW
I have reviewed the requested activity in Section I and determined that (X and complete as applicable)

a. FAA/OTHER GOVERNMENTAL WAIVER/LICENSE IS NOT REQUIRED.	
b. WAIVER/LICENSE IS REQUIRED FOR THE FOLLOWING EVENT(S) LISTED IN SECTION I: (Specify)	
c. COORDINATION HAS BEEN ACCOMPLISHED WITH CONTROLLING AIR TRAFFIC CONTROL FACILITY.	
d. AIR TRAFFIC COORDINATION IS NOT REQUIRED.	
e. DEMONSTRATION SITE FEASIBILITY STUDY IS REQUIRED. (Must meet show line, crowd line, airspace parameters.)	
f. DEMONSTRATION SITE FEASIBILITY STUDY IS NOT REQUIRED.	

16. FEASIBILITY DETERMINATION Based upon my review of this site, I find the site to be: (X one)	SATISFACTORY	UNSATISFACTORY

NOTE: If the show site is marked "Unsatisfactory," the request for the applicable activity cannot be accepted by the Department of Defense.

17. ADDITIONAL COMMENTS (Mandatory if FARs are waived)

18. COORDINATING OFFICIAL

a. NAME (Last, First, Middle Initial)	b. FLIGHT STANDARDS DISTRICT OFFICE	c. TELEPHONE NO. (Include area code)
d. SIGNATURE		e. DATE SIGNED (YYMMMDD)

DD FORM 2535, AUG 94

Page 2 of 4 Pages

A-2

SECTION V - PROGRAM			
19. PROGRAM THEME AND OBJECTIVE			

20. CHARGES AND FEES

a. ADMISSION	b. PARKING	c. SEATING	d. OTHER (Specify)
e. DOES EVENT RAISE FUNDS? (X one) ☐ YES (Complete 20.f. and 20.g.) ☐ NO	f. FUNDS WILL BE USED FOR (X as applicable) ☐ (1) CHARITIES ☐ (2) EXPENSES ☐ (3) PRIZES ☐ (4) OTHER		g. SPECIFIC INSTRUCTIONS FOR USE OF FUNDS

21. HISTORICAL INFORMATION

a. LIST ALL YEARS THE EVENT WAS HELD	b. LAST AERIAL DEMONSTRATION AND YEAR OF PERFORMANCE (i.e., Blue Angels, Thunderbirds, Golden Knights)		c. CIVILIAN AND MILITARY AIRCRAFT AT LAST YEAR'S EVENT

SECTION VI - SUPPORT (All requests other than Flyovers)	
22. THE SPONSOR AGREES TO: (Initial each item signifying acceptance. Lack of initials renders the event ineligible for all support other than Flyovers.)	**INITIALS**
a. OBTAIN THE AIR SHOW WAIVER FROM THE FAA MONITOR PRIOR TO THE EVENT FOR EACH ACTIVITY REQUIRING A WAIVER (plan a 60-day lead time). FAILURE TO OBTAIN A WAIVER WILL RESULT IN DEMONSTRATION CANCELLATION AT THE EXPENSE OF THE SPONSOR.	
b. PROVIDE AERIAL PHOTOGRAPH AND AIRFIELD DIAGRAM UPON REQUEST.	
c. PAY TEAM COSTS AS OUTLINED ON PAGE 4, PARAGRAPHS 6 OR 8 OF INSTRUCTIONS, AS APPLICABLE.	
d. PROVIDE OR REIMBURSE TRANSPORTATION, MEALS, AND QUARTERS COSTS (including pre-event visits) FOR ARMED FORCES PARTICIPANTS, AS REQUIRED. (Reimbursement for demonstration teams covered in paragraphs 6 or 8 of Instructions.)	
e. PROVIDE TELEPHONE FACILITIES FOR NECESSARY OFFICIAL COMMUNICATIONS AT THE EVENT SITE.	
f. PROVIDE MOBILE FIREFIGHTING, CRASH, AND GROUND-TO-AIR COMMUNICATIONS EQUIPMENT AT THE SHOW SITE FOR FLIGHT AND PARACHUTE DEMONSTRATIONS AND STATIC DISPLAY AIRCRAFT.	
g. PROVIDE SUITABLE AIRCRAFT FUEL AT MILITARY CONTRACT PRICES. (Sponsor must pay all costs over military contract prices, including any transportation and handling charges, if fuel is not available at such prices.)	
h. PROVIDE SECURITY FOR AIRCRAFT AT EVENT SITE DURING ENTIRE STAY.	
i. PROVIDE AMBULANCE AND MEDICAL PERSONNEL ON SITE DURING FLIGHT AND PARACHUTE DEMONSTRATIONS AND CERTAIN OTHER TYPES OF AERIAL ACTIVITIES AS DETERMINED, IN ADVANCE, BY THE MILITARY SERVICES OR OASD (PUBLIC AFFAIRS).	

SECTION VII - CERTIFICATION BY SPONSOR	
23. PRESIDENT/CHAIRMAN OF SPONSORING ORGANIZATION/BASE OR WING COMMANDER (If military sponsored)	
I certify that the information provided above is complete and accurate to the best of my knowledge. I understand that representatives from the military services will contact us to discuss arrangements and additional costs involved prior to final commitments. Any changes to the information on this form may invalidate eligibility for military participation.	
a. SIGNATURE	b. DATE SIGNED (YYMMMDD)

DD FORM 2535, AUG 94

Page 3 of 4 Pages

INSTRUCTIONS

1. The attached form is used to request U.S. Armed Forces aircraft participation at public events (maximum of 3 days) in support of community relations programs held outside a military installation, and for requesting an aerial demonstration team (U.S. Army Golden Knights, U.S. Navy Blue Angels, or U.S. Air Force Thunderbirds) to perform on or off a military installation, worldwide. Civilian sponsors must use this form in all instances, while military sponsors need only use this form when requesting performances by the Golden Knights, Blue Angels, or the Thunderbirds (includes joint-use airfields/facilities). This form is used by DoD to determine eligibility of an event for military aerial support. Once an event has been approved as eligible, it is the event sponsor's responsibility, working through the individual Service public affairs offices, to gain support.

2. The event sponsor is responsible for gaining the completion of Section IV, FAA Coordination, prior to submission of the form to DoD. The local Flight Standards District Office which has jurisdiction over the event site will complete all appropriate blocks in Section IV. Requests for static displays only do not require FAA coordination. Complete Sections I - III and V - VII, and forward the form to the nearest Flight Standards District Office (FSDO) for completion of Section IV.

3. The local sponsoring organization is responsible for the accurate completion of the form and conducting the event. The information on this form must be typed or printed in ink, and is used to evaluate the event for compliance with public law and Department of Defense policies, and to determine its eligibility for Armed Forces participation. In all cases, military participation must not interfere with military operations and training programs, and must be at no additional cost to the U.S. Government. Sponsors will consult with local military recruiters and provide, at no charge, prime space at the event site for recruiting activities. Department of Defense is unable to support events for which sponsorship is intended to make a business profit. Events which have an admission charge, or other associated charges, do not necessarily preclude military participation. Military commands cannot participate in events which charge admission unless the military participation is incidental to the event, and not the primary attraction. Incomplete forms, or forms submitted late, cannot be considered and will be returned to the sponsor's representative.

4. Requests for flyovers will be considered only if the event is aviation oriented (i.e., air shows, airport anniversaries or dedication events), or for patriotic observances (1 day only) held in conjunction with Armed Forces Day, Memorial Day, Independence Day, POW/MIA Recognition Day, or Veterans Day (event must be within seven days of the actual holiday date to be considered). Flyovers may be performed by operational or training aircraft as determined by the Services. Sponsors of events other than bona fide air shows are prohibited from scheduling more than one Service to conduct the flyover. Once confirmation of Service participation is gained, other Services will not participate in the event. The Blue Angels, Thunderbirds, and the Marine Corps do not perform flyovers. Requests for flyovers must be received for processing at least 90 days prior to the event for full consideration by the Services. Requests received closer than 90 days may not allow adequate planning for some organizations to support. Requests received 30 days or closer will not be considered. Flyover requests for formal observances of the stated patriotic holidays (no more than four of the same type aircraft making a single pass) may be forwarded to a Service command or a military installation public affairs office. Complete Sections I - III and V - VII, and forward the form to the nearest Flight Standards District Office (FSDO) for completion of Section IV. The missing man formation will not be flown in support of any activities requested on this form. It is reserved for funeral services in honor of active duty rated/designated aviators or dignitaries of the Federal Government or as determined by the Military Services.

5. Requests for aircraft static displays will only be considered for air shows, airport events, expositions and fairs, and public events which contribute to the public knowledge of Armed Forces equipment and capabilities (including recruiting and ROTC events). Complete Sections I - III and V - VII (Section IV is not applicable when requesting static displays only). Requests may be sent from the sponsoring organization to OASD(PA) Directorate for Community Relations (DCR), a Service command public affairs office, or directly to a military installation public affairs office at least 90 days prior to the event for full consideration by all Services. The sponsor must satisfy all safety and operational requirements for the requested aircraft. Requests received closer than 90 days may not allow adequate planning for some organizations to support. Requests received 30 days or closer will not be considered.

6. Civilian-sponsored requests for performances by a flight demonstration team (Blue Angels and Thunderbirds) will be considered only for events which are: (1) aviation oriented (i.e., air shows, airport events, historical aviation events); (2) planning civilian aviation participation; (3) open to all Military Services for participation; and (4) held during the air show season (mid-March to mid-November). A partial reimbursement cost (quarters and meals) of $6,000 per official demonstration (including any performance where admission is charged to view a team) is payable by all nonmilitary sponsors as indicated in the team support manual. Appearances on a military installation or sponsored by a military organization will only be approved in support of an official installation "open house" program (no admission charge/entrance fee). All event sponsors are required to comply with all aspects of the team support manual, as applicable. All requests for an aerial demonstration team must be received by OASD(PA)DCR by August 1 of the year preceding the year of the event. Complete Sections I - III and V - VII, and forward the form to the nearest Flight Standards District Office (FSDO) for completion of Section IV. The annual schedule will be released in December of the year prior to the season. Subsequent to public release of the schedule, teams will be rescheduled if a scheduled event is cancelled, the original sponsoring organization is changed, or the original event site is changed. Previously validated requests will automatically be reconsidered. NOTE: Blue Angels and Thunderbirds require 8,000 and 7,000 foot runways, respectively, at or within 30-50 nautical miles of the demonstration site. The Blue Angels also require arresting gear located within 80 nautical miles of the demonstration site.

7. Requests for single aircraft demonstrations (i.e., F-15, F-14, Harrier) will be considered for events as described in paragraph 6 (1) through (4) above. Requests for single aircraft demonstrations must be approved by OASD(PA)DCR. Army, Navy, and Air Force single aircraft demonstrations must be received for processing at least 90 days prior to the event. Harrier (AV-8B) demonstrations must be received by January 31 each year. (Scheduled Harrier events will receive two aircraft, one for demonstration and one for static display. Fifty gallons of distilled water must be provided for each Harrier demonstration.) Meals, lodging, and transportation for the aircrew must be provided by the sponsor.

8. Civilian-sponsored requests for the U.S. Army Parachute Team, the Golden Knights, will be considered for events such as air shows, airport dedications and anniversaries, expositions and fairs, events sponsored by the Army, and those events which contribute to the public knowledge of military and airborne operations, equipment and capabilities. All requests must be received by OASD(PA)DCR by October 1 of the year preceding the year of the event. Appearances on a military installation will only be approved in support of an official "open house" program. All sponsors, military and civilian, are required to reimburse the team for quarters, meals, ground transportation, and a designated rate for the jump platform (aircraft), as determined by the team, at least two weeks prior to the event (approximately $3,500 per official show day). The annual schedule will be released (approximately January-February approximately 45 days after the flight demonstration teams' schedules). After the official schedule is released, the Golden Knights will consider "add on" performances if received by OASD(PA)DCR at least 60 days prior to the date of the event. In the event of cancellations, all requests previously validated will automatically be reconsidered. Complete Sections I - III and V - VII, and forward the form to the nearest Flight Standards District Office (FSDO) for completion of Section IV.

9. Additional forms may be obtained through the office listed below or through the nearest military installation public affairs office. Check with the office below for changes to the form. If you have questions regarding the information on this form, please call the Directorate for Community Relations between 8:30 a.m. and 5:00 p.m. Eastern Time, Monday through Friday, holidays excepted.

Commercial: (703) 695-9368
DSN: 225-9368
FAX: (703) 695-4323

MAIL COMPLETED FORM TO:

Aviation Liaison Officer
Directorate for Community Relations, Room 1E776
1400 Defense Pentagon
Washington, DC 20301-1400

SPONSOR: PLEASE RETAIN A COPY OF THIS FORM FOR FUTURE REFERENCE.

DD FORM 2535, AUG 94

APPENDIX B

AV-8B HARRIER AIRSHOW REQUIREMENTS CHECKLIST

The AV-8B Harrier is a unique, sophisticated aircraft with support demands which often differ from those of other aircraft which participate in public events. Final approval of Harrier demonstration support for an airshow is contingent on the sponsor's ability to meet these different support requirements.

Please complete the following checklist concerning your ability to provide the required support and forward it to the squadron providing the demonstration.

FUEL: JP-5 or Jet A fuel is required for the AV-8B. If neither are on hand, arrangements should be made to secure sufficient quantities for some other source. For a two-day airshow (two demonstrations) and for one practice demonstration, a total of about 3,000 gallons is needed. The pilots and plane captain are not authorized to pay for fuel. If the fuel is not available under a government contract, the sponsor is required to pay the difference between the current government contract rate and the commercial rate. In the case of civilian sponsors, the Navy Fiscal Office will forward payment at a date subsequent to the airshow.

Will JP-5 or Jet Alpha fuel be available at the event site?

_____

If JP-5 or Jet Alpha fuel is not available on site, what arrangements will be made to provide either type?

_____

_____

DEMINERALIZED WATER: Approximately 50 gallons of demineralized or distilled water per demonstration are required for engine cooling and increased lift during vertical maneuvers of the Harrier.

Will 50 gallons of demineralized/distilled water be made available at the event site?

_____

SAFETY SERVICE: It is essential that adequate crash and rescue facilities, mobile firefighting, and medical services be available during all Harrier performances (including the rehearsal). Fire fighting equipment must include CO_2 extinguishers since other chemicals will corrode the aircraft. An ambulance with qualified personnel must also be available during the flight demonstrations.

Indicate safety services to be provided:

_____

_____

SECURITY: Twenty-four hour security for the aircraft is MANDATORY. In the case of a civilian show site, the security personnel must have legal authority to apprehend civilians. Military personnel do not have such authority.

Will 24-hour security be provided?

_____

Indicate the type of security force to be provided:

_____

DEMONSTRATION SITE: The site for the hover and vertical take-off and landing portions of the demonstration must be composed of a marked concrete runway to provide visual indicators. There can be NO cracks or chips in the surface. Without a concrete surface, vertical landings or take-offs will NOT be demonstrated. It *is requested that the sponsor provide photographs and schematics of the demonstration site to the squadron when the checklist is returned.* Also indicate the following:

Type of surface? _____

Forecasted temperatures/pressure altitude?

_____

Elevation at site? _____

FAA WAIVER: FAA waivers are required for the Harrier demonstrations for each airshow and for the required practice demonstration which is normally accomplished on the day prior to the show. Requests for waivers are to be submitted to the nearest General Aviation District Office on FAA Form 77112 (Application for Certification of Waiver or Authorization).

The area of operation to be requested in the waiver is 3000 feet AGL within a 5-nautical mile radius of the airport. The FAA requires that the waiver request be submitted at least 60 days prior to the airshow. It is not always possible, however, to notify sponsors of the availability of the Harrier in time to meet the deadline. If a Harrier demonstration has not been confirmed by 60 days prior to the event, it is recommended that the sponsor initiate an FAA waiver application pending final response to the request. In the past, some FAA offices have approved late requests if waivers have been granted for other aerial demonstrations in the airshow.

Has an FAA waiver been requested for each Harrier demonstration? _____

If a waiver has not yet been requested, on what date will it be requested? _____

CREW ACCOMMODATIONS: Marine participants in public events are not reimbursed by the government for expenses incurred away from their home bases. Therefore, airshow sponsors, civilian or military, are required to defray those expenses by providing one good hotel/motel room per crewmember, meals and local transportation for the two pilots and for the enlisted plane captain upon their arrival at the airshow site.

Indicate your plans for crew lodging, meals and transportation: _____
_____
_____

GROUND CREWMEMBER (Civilian Air Fields ONLY): Airshow sponsors must provide for round trip transportation, at no expense to the government, for the enlisted plane captain from the Harrier squadron to assist the pilots in servicing and maintenance of the aircraft. An airline ticket for travel to and from the airshow site should be delivered to the participating squadron at least one week prior to the date of the airshow. Arrangements should be made by direct liaison between the airshow sponsor and the Harrier squadron.

Will round-trip transportation, meals and lodging be provided at no expense to the government or enlisted plane captain for his participation? _____

ARRIVAL OF AIRCREW: Upon arrival at the airshow site, the pilots and plane captain should be provided schedules of all briefings/rehearsal and details concerning aircraft parking and security.

What is the designated arrival time for the pilots/plane captain prior to rehearsal? _____

_____

_____

MEDIA PLAN: A media packet will be mailed to the airshow sponsors upon notification of a scheduled Harrier demonstration. The packet will contain 8x10 photos and a fact sheet. Video clips are available upon request. Sponsors are asked to coordinate with the local Marine recruiters in releasing these materials to the appropriate media outlets.

Public appearances and/or media interviews with the pilots on the day prior to the airshow may be arranged in some instances. Inquiries regarding such appearances/interviews should be directed to the respective Harrier squadron providing the demonstration approximately two weeks prior to the scheduled demonstrations. Often times, the pilots are not assigned until days prior to the demonstration.

Briefly describe your media plan for the Harrier demonstration: _____

_____

_____

STATIC DISPLAY: Two Harriers will be assigned to each airshow. One will function as the demonstration aircraft while the other is intended for static display. Airshow sponsors are asked to arrange placement of the display aircraft in a prominent location at the airshow site if feasible, allowing maximum visibility to the spectators. It is also requested that space be reserved adjacent to the static display aircraft for a Marine Corps recruiting booth/van.

Indicate your plans for displaying the second Harrier:

_____

_____

_____

Indicate your plans to include a Marine Corps recruiter's
booth in the display: _____

_____

_____

The AV-8B Harrier is scheduled for participation in air
shows as operational and training commitments permit. The
Marine Corps does not have a "demo team" specifically designated
as a flight demonstration aircraft. Please note that a Harrier
demonstration is contingent upon the airshow's ability to provide
the above-mentioned support. Should any problems arise, please
contact the cognizant Harrier squadron or Headquarters Marine
Corps, Division of Public Affairs, Community Relations Branch
at (703) 614-1034/54.

APPENDIX C

AIRSHOW AFTER ACTION REPORT

SUBJ/AIRSHOW AFTER ACTION REPORTING PROCEDURES
1.   THE QUESTIONNAIRE OUTLINED IN PAR 2 OF THIS REF MUST BE
COMPLETED BY AIRCREWS WHO PARTICIPATE IN AIRSHOW STATIC DISPLAY
OR FLIGHT DEMONSTRATIONS.
2.   FLIGHT DEMO/STATIC DISPLAY AFTER ACTION QUESTIONNAIRE:
FROM: (AVIATION UNIT)
TO: CMC WASHINGTON DC//ASM/PA/MCRC//
VIA:
SUBJ: AIRSHOW AFTER ACTION REPORT
1.   IN ACCORDANCE WITH THE REFERENCE, THE FOLLOWING IS SUBMITTED:
A.   EVENT   LOCATION   SPONSOR
B.   NUMBER/TYPE OF AIRCRAFT
C.   WAS THE AIRSHOW COORDINATOR PRESENT AND HELPFUL?
D.   WAS A MARINE RECRUITER'S BOOTH PRESENT? WAS IT CLOSE TO THE
AIRCRAFT ON DISPLAY? DID HE CONTACT YOU? DID YOU REFER ANYONE
TO HIM FOR INFO ON JOINING THE MARINE CORPS?
E.   WAS THE MEDIA IN ATTENDANCE? IF SO, WHAT TYPE(PRINT, RADIO,
TELEVISION)?
F.   WERE YOU INTERVIEWED BY THE MEDIA? IF SO, BY WHOM? FOR
PRINT? FOR BROADCAST?
G.   WERE YOU OR YOUR AIRCRAFT FILMED BY THE MEDIA?
H.   HAS THE UNIT PREVIOUSLY ATTENDED THIS EVENT?
I.   WAS THE EVENT WORTHWHILE?
J.   ESTIMATED CROWD SIZE_____.   ESTIMATED CROWD AGE_____.
K.   WAS ADEQUATE AIRCRAFT SERVICE PROVIDED?
L.   WAS SECURITY ADEQUATE?
M.   WAS YOUR AIRCRAFT ROPED OFF?
N.   WAS SMOKING ALLOWED ON THE FLIGHT LINE?
O.   HOW WAS OVERALL CROWD CONTROL?
P.   WERE THE ATC FACILITIES HELPFUL?
Q.   LIST ANY NOTEWORTHY UNSAFE TRENDS/EVENTS.
R.   WAS BILLETING PROVIDED? ADEQUATE? ON BASE?
S.   WAS FOOD PROVIDED? ADEQUATE? ON BASE?
T.   WAS TRANSPORTATION PROVIDED? ADEQUATE?
U.   IN YOUR OPINION, SHOULD THE MARINE CORPS CONTINUE TO SUPPORT
THIS AIRSHOW? STATE REASONS (I.E., WAS IT A BENEFIT TO
RECRUITING EFFORTS?) AIRCREW SIGNATURE.
3. COMPLETE THE QUESTIONNAIRE AND SUBMIT BY MSG TO CMC
WASHINGTON DC//ASM/PA/MCRC// NLT 5 WORKING DAYS FOLLOWING AIRSHOW
PARTICIPATION.

www.ingramcontent.com/pod-product-compliance
Lightning Source LLC
Chambersburg PA
CBHW080904290526
45795CB00007BA/2397